The Bible is filled with stories of heroes and champions of long ago, used by God in difficult and dangerous times, to bring rescue and deliverance to oppressed and marginalized people, in the Name of Jesus.

In *Go Back: The Power of Obedience*, Pastor Oleksandr Ilash and his ministry team embody the story of modern-day Christian faith and courage, on display and under great personal risk. In the midst of a devastating international crisis of war and carnage, God is using them to bring effective, holistic ministry to thousands in Christ's name in the besieged nation of Ukraine.

The Apostolic Faith Church in Chicago is grateful to God for their ongoing, courageous demonstration of faith. We stand committed with our prayerful and financial support to their God-glorifying efforts. We urge others to also undergird them and stand in faith, that God will continue to grant them divine covering and favor as He uses them in this heroic work.

> Bishop Horace E. Smith
> Senior Pastor, Apostolic Faith Church
>   (Chicago, IL, USA)
> Former Presiding Bishop, Pentecostal
>   Assemblies of the World, Inc.

****

Pastor Oleksandr Ilash shares his journey on how being obedient to the voice of God within a war-torn nation exemplifies what the focus of a soul winner should be. This book illustrates the sensitivity of a man of God on a mission and paints a vivid and captivating picture of truth in action that every soul matters.

> Bishop Michael D. Franklin
> European Council of Nations East
> Pentecostal Assemblies of the World, Inc.

I am privileged to have met Pastor Oleksandr Ilash (Pastor Alex) in 2022. He was introduced virtually as a youthful and dynamic pastor who was assisting people in Ukraine to escape to safer territories in neighboring countries as Russia invaded. I was so impressed that I asked the bishops gathering in Tampa, Florida, for our spring conference meetings to have a special prayer time for this young man's efforts. Before we dismissed Pastor Alex from the virtual social media platform, the Holy Spirit led me to personally guarantee him financial assistance from my church and partners with a certain amount of money.

As I got to know him and began to share videos of his humanitarian efforts—which demonstrated courage and a perfect mix of spiritual and natural assistance to people who were experiencing grave dangers—finances began to pour in, exceeding our expectations. The collected amount was three times larger than what I had pledged to give.

Let me introduce you to Pastor Alex, a modern-day Nehemiah. I know you will be blessed and encouraged to answer the call of God in your own life as you read what this young man has done and is continuing to do.

Bishop Charles H. Ellis III
Senior Pastor, Greater Grace Temple
(Detroit, MI, USA)
Former Presiding Bishop

****

Pastor Oleksandr's call in Ukraine began when he obeyed God after he thought he was secure and living apart from his beloved country with his family. *Go Back* tells the story of Pastor Alex returning home amidst bombs, drones, mines, death, and destruction. His determination to stay and serve his people is a wonderful example of the church's role in these last days. This book is a must-read for all in Christian service.

Bishop Richard D. Howell Jr.
Senior Pastor, Shiloh Temple International
Ministries (Minneapolis, MN, USA)
Second Assistant Presiding Bishop, Pentecostal
Assemblies of the World, Inc.

Go Back
by Oleksandr Ilash
Copyright ©2023 Oleksandr Ilash

ISBN 978-1-63360-275-5

All rights reserved under International Copyright Law. Written permission must be secured from the publisher/author to reproduce, copy, or transmit any part of this book.

Unless otherwise noted, all scripture quotations taken from the Holy Bible, New International Version©, NIV©. Copyright © 1973, 1978; 1984, 2011 by Biblica, Inc." Used by permission of Zondervan. All rights reserved world-wide. www.zondervan.com The "NIV" and "New International Version" are trademarks registered in the United States Patent and Trademark Office by Biblica, Inc.

For Worldwide Distribution
Printed in the U.S.A.

Urban Press
P.O. Box 8881
Pittsburgh, PA 15221-0881 USA
412.646.2780
www.urbanpress.us

TABLE OF CONTENTS

ACKNOWLEDGMENTS   **VII**
PRAYER FOR UKRAINE   **X**
INTRODUCTION   **XI**

CHAPTER 1
ADVICE   **1**

CHAPTER 2
GO BACK   **7**

CHAPTER 3
THE BORDER   **19**

CHAPTER 4
OPEN DOORS   **29**

CHAPTER 5
ADAPTING TO CHANGING NEEDS   **41**

CHAPTER 6
GREEN CARD   **57**

CHAPTER 7
PRESERVATION   **65**

CHAPTER 8
PERSONAL IMPACT   **77**

CHAPTER 9
REFLECTIONS ON THE WAR   **83**

HOW YOU CAN HELP   **88**
CONTACT INFO   **91**

ACKNOWLEDGMENTS

First and foremost, I extend my heartfelt gratitude to my precious wife. Despite her fears, she stood unwaveringly by my side, supporting my decision to heed the voice of God and return to the war-torn country of Ukraine to begin a new ministry. Her steadfast love and strength have been the bedrock of this journey, and I am truly blessed to have her as my partner.

I am immensely thankful to the exceptional individuals and organizations who, despite their own projects and needs, generously responded to the needs and cries of the Ukrainian people, surpassing our expectations:

Presiding Bishop Theodore L. Brooks Sr., and all the Pentecostal Assemblies of the World (PAW) churches

Bishop Horace E. Smith, Senior Pastor, Apostolic Faith Church (Chicago, IL, USA)

Go Back

Bishop Charles H. Ellis III, Senior Pastor,
Greater Grace Temple (Detroit, MI, USA)

Bishop Richard D. Howell Jr., Senior Pastor,
Shiloh Temple International Ministries
(Minneapolis, MN, USA)

Bishop Michael D. Franklin,
European Council of Nations East, PAW, Inc.

Pastors Michael and Tami Keller and all the
Apostolic Ministers Alliance (AMA) churches
(Grand Rapids, MI, USA)

Pastor Luke Smith and all the Apostolic World
Christian Fellowship (AWCF) churches

Pastor David Goudy,
Moira Pentecostal Church (Northern Ireland)

Pastor George Hancock,
Christian World Church (Dallas, TX, USA)

Pastor Dee Jay Shoulders and all the Associated
Brotherhood of Christians churches (USA)

Stefan Radelich and all the
Feed the Hungry (FTH) staff and volunteers.

Last, but certainly not least, I wish to express my heartfelt thanks and the highest respect to the four individuals who encouraged me to write this book and helped transfer these stories and testimonies onto paper for all of you who are reading it now. Without these remarkable people, this book would never have seen the light of day:

My dear creative brother,
Dan Ilash (ilashcreative.com)

The honorable Dr. Horace Smith
(Apostolic Faith Church, Chicago, IL, USA)

Dearest Bishop Michael D. Franklin,
European Council of Nations East, PAW, Inc.

The phenomenal man and publisher,
Dr. John Stanko, of Urban Press.

Your unwavering support and encouragement have made this book a reality, and I am profoundly grateful for each and every one of you. May the impact of our collective efforts bring inspiration and positive change to those who read these pages.

SPECIAL ACKNOWLEDGMENT

The publisher and author would like to acknowledge the outstanding work of Urban Press intern Jenna Wright who worked tirelessly to compile, arrange, and edit this manuscript. We are grateful for your efforts, Jenna, and look forward to working with you again.

PRAYER FOR UKRAINE

BY DR. JOHN STANKO

Father, we pray for Alex and his team, that You would continue to use them to spread the light of Your Word and the light of Your love to people who are under such difficult circumstances. We pray for Alex's family, that you would minister to them as well. We pray for resources, Lord, and that You will use this and other connections and contacts that he's made to provide for the work that You are doing in Ukraine. Watch over them all, Lord; protect them. I know they will give You the honor and glory. Help us to know how to tell the story well, so that it will tell of the work that You're doing and the work that they're doing to carry out the practical steps of Your love to a people in great need. In Jesus' name, we pray. Amen.

INTRODUCTION

My name is Alex Ilash, and I am a pastor in Izmail, Ukraine. I'm 33 years old. I've been married to my wife, Anastasia, for 12 years. We have two wonderful children: Joseph, who is 10, and Lika, who is nine. I've been in the ministry pretty much all of my life. I was born into a Christian family. From an early age, I had a good example of how to serve God from my parents, who were founders of the Well of Living Water Church in the city of Izmail in the very south of Ukraine, and from other pastors there. In 2008 I was baptized in Jesus' name. Later in the same year, I went to Bible college at New Generation. I cultivated a deeper understanding of God's Word and a stronger relationship with Christ during my time there.

In 2009 I was blessed to start a youth ministry in our church. I still preached on Sundays a couple of times a month, but mainly my life was dedicated to being a youth minister. For 13 years I ran the youth ministry, and by the grace of God, I was able to build a youth center on our church property. That center is still running and operating. Sometimes it's very hard to get young people to church. The youth center is an intermediate place for them—something between the non-Christian world and the church—where we build relationships with young people and invite them to youth services every Saturday. We spend time with them and help them start their new life with Jesus.

All my life has been about reaching people outside of the church walls—preaching the gospel to them and running programs to engage them toward the church. This was my wife's and my life since we were married, and even before our marriage. I am located in Izmail, but I sometimes travel to the United States to raise support for the ministry here. I am able to do this because I learned English in a school in Ukraine. I practice interpreting for people who come to my church and for my father while we travel in the U.S.

Our church has always been what I would call an outdoor church, meaning that we try our best to do a lot of things outside of the church walls. Sometimes, for huge holidays like Christmas, Easter, and Thanksgiving Day, we sponsor some activity in the city, especially for the young people. In the month of August, we do a "Back-to-School" event with water slides and food, and we distribute a lot of school supplies to kids. We've done this for many years, but since the war began, we mostly focus on helping the children of internally displaced people, as well as children from our city.

Our church also expanded its ministry to other parts of Ukraine after the first Russian invasion in 2014, when Russia conquered Crimea and the eastern part of our country. Starting at that time, I was part of a team from our church—consisting of my dad, a couple of other church brothers, and me—who made humanitarian trips to affected areas. We used our church vans to deliver food, aid, and different supplies. The need in that area was high back in those days. It was a great opportunity to help people and tell them about Christ. Overall, we completed fifteen missionary trips to eastern Ukraine over several years.

When the war hit our country in 2022, by the grace of God, I was able to move my family outside of Ukraine—a story I will relate in Chapter Two. Then the Lord called me to come back to Ukraine and start the same humanitarian efforts in my own region, based out of my church. The Lord provided the opportunity, resources, and desire to do this outreach of helping refugees and other internally displaced people in our area, which we estimate to be about 50,000 people.

Our efforts include feeding the people and providing them with supplies, such as medication, diapers for their kids, nutrition, clothes, bed clothing, and other basic supplies they need. Keep in mind, these people have lost everything. We are also using the opportunity created by this situation to preach the gospel to them and share about our loving Jesus and how our God cares for them—even while war ravages the country. They need to know that He really cares and loves them. This is the main emphasis of our ministry and mission: to feed the hungry, but also to tell them about Jesus.

My church has been doing this since the beginning of the war, sometimes supplying food and provisions for up to 350 people every day. At one point, we were taking care of meals not just for the refugees, but also for the local police and the military. Wherever we see the need, we are trying to meet it. We minister to display the real love of Christ in practical ways, attempting to show people what Christianity is about.

I wrote this book to build your faith and show that even in the midst of your circumstances God is moving, and He is able to do miraculous things in your life and the lives of your loved ones. Along the way, I will also share my family's story, how we started the refugee ministry, and various testimonies from people who have been impacted by our efforts.

Back in February 2022, most of the population in my country was skeptical about the possibility of a Russian invasion. Even though my family and I had made those humanitarian trips to eastern Ukraine from 2015 to 2018 and had seen the reality of that Russian invasion, we also were hesitant to believe the rumors. We had seen the devastation with our own eyes and had talked to the people there. But for some reason, we thought that this was something that had happened long ago and would not happen again in 2022.

I thought that world leaders would not allow Putin to invade a sovereign country. I thought that Putin wouldn't dare do that. United States intelligence had warned our leadership of the impending invasion as early as November of 2021, a few months before it happened. They said it looked like Putin was gathering his troops, tanks, and artillery all along the northeast border. The Russians were saying that they were just conducting a military exercise, but some suspected they were going to invade the country and that Putin would try to conquer the rest of Ukraine. However, most of us thought this was nonsense and that it was not going to happen.

This is how my story begins. As you read, I ask that you pray for my country, for our ministry, and for the people with whom we are working. If your heart moves you to help us financially, the information for how to do so is at the end of the book. But for now, let's begin the story of *Go Back: The Power of Obedience*.

CHAPTER 1

ADVICE

Early in January 2022, I attended a Christian political conference in the capital of my country, the city of Kyiv. Between the sessions, there was a lunch break. When people ask, I always tell them that the people in Ukraine are pretty much the same as people in the United States: everyone enjoys lunch breaks! I was enjoying that break and visiting with many people, and I ended up having a conversation with a pastor named Kirill Bondarenko. He and I discussed a number of things about family and church. Then he surprised me by asking me a question: "Alex, how are you and your people in Izmail preparing yourselves for a possible Russian invasion?"

That was an unexpected question. As I said in the introduction, in 2015 our church had delivered a lot of supplies and food to the eastern section of our country that Russia had already conquered. Even though I had seen the reality of Russian aggression,

Go Back

I never imagined that the same horror would engulf the rest of Ukraine in 2022.

I responded to him, "Pastor, to be honest, we don't really believe that Putin would dare invade. We don't believe it's going to happen. That's why we are doing nothing to prepare ourselves."

When I said that, he looked at me sternly and seriously and said, "Alex, I'm going to give you some advice. These are a few points, very simple things, but I really hope you're going to hear me and do this for your family.

"When you're back home in your city, pack your traveling suitcases for your wife, your kids, and yourself with some of your most needed items for travel. Then please confirm you know where your passports are for you and your family, and that they aren't expired, so you'll be ready for travel. Next, withdraw some money so you have cash in hand, and make sure the gasoline tank of your car is always filled with fuel."

That was his advice. I looked at him and replied, "But why? Why do I need to do these things?"

He answered, "Alex, we have some experience based on what happened to our country in 2014. When Russia invaded, it was chaos. There was panic all around. People wanted to move their families outside of the country and tried to get some gas to do so. They tried to get some money from the ATMs. But in just two hours, there was no gas at the gas stations, and in just three hours, there was no money in the ATMs. You don't want to face these obstacles on your way to leaving the country. I'm telling you, Alex, if Russia invades, you will want to move your family outside of Ukraine immediately. You have no idea what Russian soldiers will do to civilian people, especially to women and children. You will want to move your family outside of this country to a safe place."

Today when I share this story and tell people about this advice that I got from Pastor Kirill, it sounds really reasonable. It makes sense now, but only because we're looking at the situation through the perspective of what has happened already. But I remind you, we were skeptical at the time. I was skeptical. When Pastor Kirill shared his advice, I thought, *Wow, this is just a scared pastor. He is a scared man and has little faith.* I wondered, *Where is his faith?*

I didn't say any of that to him; they were just my thoughts. However, only two hours after I dismissed his advice and while I was still at the conference, I heard a voice inside my heart speaking to me. Now I know it was the voice of God. The voice asked me just one question: "Why wouldn't you do what he tells you, Alex?"

I started thinking about it: *Okay, Alex, is it really hard for you to pack some bags for you and your kids and your wife? This is simple. Is it really hard for you to withdraw some money and have it in cash? No, it's not. Is it really hard for you to refuel your car with gasoline every hundred miles you drive? These are all easy things. So why wouldn't you do what he tells you, Alex?* Those were the questions inside of me.

The next day I drove back to my city, Izmail, from the conference and was still skeptical and hesitant. But I completed all of those instructions because of the voice that had spoken to me. I shared the advice with some friends, relatives, and others, but I did so cautiously because I knew they were thinking like I once was. I said to them, "Hey, I've been to Kyiv. I talked with this man, and he gave me some advice that's simple and easy to follow. I think we all ought to listen and do these things for our families."

And believe it or not, nobody took the advice too seriously. People laughed at me when I shared that I was preparing for an invasion, that my bags were packed and I was refueling my car every hundred miles. They scoffed at me and said things like, "Are you serious? How long are you going to have those bags packed in your house? How long are you planning to refuel your car after every hundred miles? That's funny! Alex, stop listening to those scared people. Stop listening to that pro-Western propaganda news. It isn't going to happen."

This whole scenario reminds me of some parallel stories from the Bible, like the story of Noah for example. God warned Noah that He was going to destroy the world, and Noah had to build an ark as the only place where he and his family could be saved. In a sense, Pastor Kirill gave me instructions similar to the ones God gave Noah. The New Testament refers to Noah as a preacher of truth, because he preached to people what God was going to do. He warned them that the ark would be the only safe place once the Flood came. We know the rest of the story. No one listened to him, and he and his family were the only ones who were saved.

The other biblical story that is similar to mine is the one concerning Lot. God sent His angels to evacuate Lot and his family from a wicked city. We read that Lot tried his best to warn his sons-in-law, but when he shared the news with them, they thought he was kidding. Therefore, only Lot and some of his other relatives were saved.

And of course, these stories and my situation in Ukraine have meaning for all Christians in these end times. We know that Jesus is coming back and what is going to happen to the world when he does. We know that the Rapture is going to take place very soon. We all have heard the Great Commission from God that we are to warn people to have their traveling bags prepared and their passports for eternal life up to date. Some of them will not believe us and may even laugh at us, but my message to all Christians today is this: don't let people's opinions stop you from doing what God has called you to do, for there is a blessing in obedience. Soon after my meeting with Pastor Kirill, my family and I were glad that we listened to him, just like Christians will be glad they listened to Jesus and heeded His warnings about the end.

One fateful February morning, just one month after the conference in Kyiv, my wife and I were awakened by telephone calls from our relatives and friends who lived in Kyiv, Odessa, and other major cities. They called us to say that war had begun and that we had been correct. They were seeing the Russian invasion with their own eyes—the troops, the tanks, and their cities being bombarded.

The vast majority of people were not prepared. They had no idea what to do or how to evacuate. They then realized the advice that I had been giving them was reasonable. It would have helped them if they had listened to me. In the same way, one day in this world, people will find out that the instructions we were given in Scripture were also true. Unfortunately for many of them, it will be too late. This should make the Great Commission all the more urgent for us as Christians. As long as we have time to speak and preach to unbelievers, we must inspire them to make peace with God through Christ.

When we preach the urgency of the Great

Commission message, people may say we are crazy. Some of them will laugh at us. Others will say that Christianity is just a nonsensical fairy tale. Some will deny Jesus' Second Coming, but I hope to inspire people through the message of this book not to be discouraged from preaching the truth. When people try to stop you from doing what God has called you to do, press on. Most of the people I spoke with thought I was foolish to prepare for an invasion. Sometimes I wondered if I was doing the right thing, but I continued. I urge you not to let the opinions of people stop you from proclaiming the truth and doing what God has called you to do.

The voice of God spoke to me in Kyiv and asked me why I wouldn't do what Pastor Kirill told me. That's how it is with faith and obedience. I knew the voice was from God, and I obeyed. When Russia invaded our country one month after that conference, we were ready—my wife, my two children, and me. We were ready, and that's how we were able to leave the country immediately, without any restrictions or difficulties on the border.

CHAPTER 2

GO BACK

I will never forget that Thursday morning, February 24, 2022, at 5:00 a.m. It was an unusual morning. If you can, imagine being awakened, not by your alarm, not by your kids, but by phone calls from your scared relatives and church friends who are calling to say, "Now we are a war-torn country. Russia has invaded our country." It was an unforgettable experience.

After we got up, my wife and I and our children lifted prayers to God. We had no idea what was going to happen to our city within the next hour, within the next days. We knew our city hadn't been bombed yet, but what was going to happen now? Were we the next to be attacked? These questions and worries kept running through our minds.

Our church was supposed to have an outreach in the city that day. We went, and some brothers and our main team set up a tent to preach to people. But what we found was that the city was in a panic. People were not ready to stop and spend time with us in that tent. I witnessed what Pastor Kirill Bondarenko had told me about the 2014 invasion. There were lines of cars miles long at the gas station, where there was a limit of purchasing 15 liters (4 gallons) of fuel. I saw lines of people at ATMs just like Pastor Kirill had said. In two or three hours, the ATMs were out of cash. There were lines in the grocery stores of people who wanted to buy food in case the supply chain was stopped, which was exactly what happened in a matter of hours.

When I returned home, I called some friends of mine in Kyiv and Odessa to confirm how serious things were and ask their advice on what I should do. They said, "Alex, if you have time and if you are prepared, evacuate your family immediately. Move them out now."

I turned to my wife and said, "We prepared for this day a month ago. The Lord warned us. Now while people are trying to get gas, money, and food, we are prepared. Our car is fueled, our bags are packed, and we have cash. I don't want to wait until it's too late or too dangerous. Let's leave Ukraine and head to Romania."

We considered Romania a safe place because it is part of NATO and is close to Izmail. It's just a couple hours' drive to the border. Before we left Izmail, I made final calls to some friends, church members, and relatives and advised them, "If you are prepared, if you can pack your bags quickly, I suggest you leave the country now. I'm leaving the country, and we can live in Romania and be there in a safe place. We can figure out what we're going to do next once we get there, but we want to evacuate our families if possible."

My wife's brother, Nikita, said, "I'm heading

to your house and coming with you." When he got there, he jumped in our car, and we started our journey.

Two people called me while we were on our way. Dan Christman from South Bend, Indiana, called to advise me to evacuate my family to Romania. I took a picture of us sitting in the car with all of our luggage, sent it to him, and said, "Here we are. That's what we're doing right now."

The second person who called us was Bishop Michael D. Franklin, a representative of the Pentecostal Assemblies of the World (PAW), Eastern European Council. He called to say, "Alex, I know you're probably busy now. You're trying to figure out what to do, but I want to let you know that the PAW will not abandon you. We'll help you. We'll extend our hand of support to you, your family, and your ministry, whatever the needs you're going to have." I told him I really appreciated that, but I was really busy packing our things and would contact him in a couple of days.

By 8:00 p.m. on the day of the invasion, we were able, by the grace of God, to leave the country. That's a very important point because we were able to cross the Ukrainian, Moldavian, and Romanian borders without any difficulties, without any special regulations and requirements. It was like any other day before the war. We crossed the border with no problems or delays. Romania has a different cellular system, so I connected through Wi-Fi in their local McDonald's. I wanted to read the news and other updates about Ukraine. I found out that almost immediately after the start of the invasion, our government issued a law saying that men 18 to 60 years of age were not allowed to leave the country. It happened right after I crossed the border.

The next day I talked with friends of mine

who are church people, and they said, "Alex, I wanted to do the same as you did and move my family to Romania. Now I'm jealous and have so much regret. We couldn't make it because...," and then they would give one of several reasons. One was they had no fuel in their car, having spent half the day in queues moving from one gas station to another, refueling their car with a four-gallon limit at each station. Another was they couldn't find their passports. Yet another was they had no money in cash and couldn't figure out how to get any. After some of them resolved those issues and made it to the border, it was too late, because by then the borders were locked down, forbidding men to cross.

Hearing all those stories, I was, and still am, very grateful to Pastor Kirill Bondarenko in Kyiv who gave me the advice at the conference, even though I was skeptical. But more than that, I was thankful for the voice of God, who warned me when I thought it was a joke and wasn't taking it seriously. And that's the story of how I left Ukraine for good—or so I thought.

The next day, I called Pastor Kirill to thank him: I said, "Pastor, I just want to thank you for that four-point piece of advice and to let you know that we are in Romania." I told him I had tried my best to share his advice with other people but that, unfortunately, most had not listened to me.

He responded, "You are one of the few people who followed my advice. I'm glad to hear that you and your family are safe now." He informed me that he had also gotten out, having moved his family from Odessa to Moldova.

A local pastor from Galaţi, Romania, Vadim Medvetski, helped us find a place to stay. He and his people helped get us settled for the first night, meeting us at that McDonald's. There we were in a new country, and God provided a person who comforted us, prayed with us, and helped us get settled.

The next day, we rented a place where we could stay for a week. I only rented it for one week because I thought the war shouldn't last longer than that. I assumed that world leaders, my president, and Putin would sit down around a table and talk out a settlement.

That night we couldn't eat. We had trouble sleeping. We watched the news 24/7 for updates about Ukraine, and they were depressing. When we saw the devastation and the Russian tanks riding through the suburbs of my capital, it was too much. I struggle to find the right words to use. We weren't disappointed; we were disgusted. This was not something that should be happening in the twenty-first century. The tanks of another country, along with their soldiers, were roaming through my country, destroying buildings and homes. The Russian military was launching missiles that were landing around our government institutions, as well as churches, hospitals, and residential areas everywhere. It was so disgusting to view it all.

But at the same time, I knew that God's grace and favor were upon me. It wasn't luck that we were able to escape my war-torn country in the nick of time, right before the borders were closed for men to cross. At that time, I knew that men who couldn't leave the country were transferring their wives and children into Romania and Moldova, where they would be safe. The fathers and brothers had to stay behind in Ukraine. I felt so blessed I could be with my wife and children in a safe place. I was so grateful to God.

Then I got a phone call from my friend Pastor George Hancock, who is from Dallas, Texas. He had

Go Back

hosted my family—my parents and some of my siblings—when they had moved to the United States five years earlier, a story which I will share in Chapter 6. Pastor George had been to Ukraine on several occasions. I shared with him more of what was going on in the country, and he was concerned.

I told him, "Pastor, I don't know what to do, because the church people staying there haven't listened to my advice. It's scary to be back in Ukraine now because they locked down the border so men can't cross. It would be terrifying for me to leave my family here in another country. I'm not sure what to do, but I'm feeling more positive that I will stay here with them. I'm not going back to Ukraine because of the situation there now."

We prayed together, and he said, "Alex, you've served the people and their needs for many years. Maybe now is a time to take care of your family, or maybe it's a time to go back, but I want you to know that I will support any decision you make."

It was very important for me to hear those words. He never said, "No, I think you have to be back in Ukraine because you're a pastor." He said, "I will support your decision. Let me know if I can somehow help you and your family."

The next day, after watching the news, I had a phone conversation with my father in the U.S., and he surprised me when he said, "I think the right thing would be for you to go back to Ukraine because our church people are there." We had a serious discussion about that, but after I hung up, I was still feeling like I was not going back to Ukraine. My father wanted me to, was almost pushing me back there, and I was thinking, *Are you serious? My wife and kids are here. How could I leave them here without me?*

After that, I was confident I would be staying someplace in Europe but was not going back to Ukraine. Then, because I was so grateful to God because of what He had done for me, I wanted to spend some time with Him in prayer. I went to the kitchen in our apartment, which became my secret, quiet room of prayer. I locked the doors, and I lifted my voice in prayer, giving my thanks to God for what he had done for my family and me.

I prayed for the people in Ukraine, especially those in our church. It was then that I had the same feeling I had had a month earlier at the conference in Kyiv. I heard the small, gentle voice once again speaking to me: it said, "I know what you feel, and I know you're grateful, but it was not for you. It was just for your wife and children, so you could settle them and know that they are safe in another country. I have another ministry for you, back in your country."

The voice went on to say, "I'm going to provide everything for that ministry. I'm going to take care of your wife and kids wherever they're going to be. I'm going to protect you, but you have to go back to Ukraine to run that new ministry there."

I wasn't ready to hear what the voice was saying. I was thinking, *Oh Lord, is this You or is this somebody else?* As a human, of course, it was scary for me to think of being back in Ukraine, especially because I had already made the decision that I was going to stay in another country in Europe.

What I have discovered through everything that has happened is the absolute importance of obeying God. There is a blessing in obedience through any circumstance, but sometimes it's easier for us to obey Him. For example, if you hear God say, "Take your family and go for a vacation to Hawaii," it is easier to obey. But sometimes, like in the story of Jonah, He may say, "Take yourself and go to Nineveh to witness to those people who are enemies of your country, who hate you. Tell them that I'm able to save them." In that situation, when God tells you to do something you don't want to do, you must obey Him anyway or otherwise find yourself stuck in a big fish's belly. It had been a blessing to be obedient to the voice I heard in Kyiv when obeying was easy, and I had to trust it would be a blessing to obey the voice I was now hearing in Romania when obeying was much harder.

I thought, *If God is speaking this to me, somehow I have to do this. But the most difficult thing will be to share this with Anastasia.* Of course, my wife didn't want me to go back to Ukraine. She was happy we were together. I knew this was going to be the most difficult discussion. I left the secret room and went to the living room, where she was watching the news on TV.

I found out that when we make the decision to obey the voice of God, to be obedient to Him and take that step, He prepares our path. When I went to talk to my wife about my decision to return to Ukraine, at that very moment, there was news on the TV about my president and about Kyiv. The anchors reported that United States intelligence had sent messages to our president's office, saying, "Mr. President, we have 100% accurate information that you and your family have become target number one for Russia. If they succeed and conquer Kyiv, they will kill you. So right now, if we have your permission and as long as we have time, we want to provide you with a safe ride out of Ukraine." They told him that he could choose any country where he wanted to go and that he would get political asylum there and find safety.

It was then that my president made his famous

speech (and I'm paraphrasing here): "I'm staying in my country with my people. If you really want to help me, if you really want to help Ukraine, send us your weapons for us to be able to fight the Russians, liberate our territories, and push the aggressors back, but I'm staying in my country." My president, Volodymyr Zelenskyy, evacuated his family, but he stayed in Ukraine.

When I heard him speaking, any hesitation I had inside my mind went away. I turned to Anastasia: "Did you hear what he said? He had the opportunity to be moved to a safe place, but he chose to stay with his people. This is pretty much the same as what I heard from God while I was praying. The Lord said that this was for you and the kids. The Lord said He has a new ministry for me in Ukraine. He's going to supply and provide everything for that ministry. He is going to take care of you and the children. He will protect me, but I have to go back to Ukraine to run that ministry."

She stopped me and asked, "What is the ministry?"

I said, "I don't know. He didn't say what it would be, but I'm confident that He wants me to be back in Ukraine." I had no idea what the ministry would be. I thought, *Maybe I will simply have to fight to liberate our territories as a soldier. Or maybe I'll have to become a military chaplain and pray for soldiers. Or perhaps I'll have to evacuate people. Maybe I'll just have to stay with the church and encourage people there.* I didn't know. Sometimes we have to take faith steps, even though we don't see the rest of the picture clearly—that's what it means to be faithful and obedient.

Then we joined hands and prayed together. Anastasia cried and said, "I hate to say this, but I feel the same way, that this is the right thing for you to do. God really wants you to be back in Ukraine. And yes, if God called you to do this, let's do it." And with tears in her eyes, she gave me a ride in our car back to the border. We took our last selfie together, having no idea when or if we would be able to see each other again in person.

She headed back to the apartment in Romania, and I started crossing the borders to get back to Ukraine, through Romania and Moldova, and finally, to Ukraine. I didn't do this because I was super brave. I didn't do it because I was crazy. No, I went because I was discovering how important it is, and what a blessing it is, to be obedient to God.

The picture I sent to Dan Christman when he suggested I evacuate my family to Romania

Final picture with Anastasia at the Ukrainian border

CHAPTER 3

THE BORDER

Altogether, I spent about 40 hours in Romania. When my family and I had crossed the Ukrainian border the first time, it was very easy to leave the country. There were no long lines and no restrictions. But in just 40 hours, everything had changed. When I made it back to the Ukrainian border, I was shocked. I saw thousands of people there, who were from all over southeast Ukraine. Our border system wasn't equipped to handle that many people at once—it just collapsed.

While crossing the border back into Ukraine, I found out that some of the refugees had been standing in line to leave the country for between 17 and 25 hours on February 26 in the freezing winter weather. They were not in a facility but rather in a field at a border checkpoint. Some of them were sitting in their cars, but so many more were standing with their children and luggage. I could see disappointment, fear, and brokenness in their eyes, like there was no sense in leaving because many of them had already lost everything. They had lost their houses, their jobs, their businesses. Many had family members who were injured or killed. They moved with a deep fear and just one desire: to leave their war-torn country and get to a safe place with their families. The men who had three or more children were eligible to leave the country.

They all were shocked to see one man with a suitcase in his hand who wanted to cross the border back into Ukraine, while all of them wanted to leave the country. Some of them said I was crazy. I remember the border officer who checked my passport. He couldn't believe that I wanted to enter Ukraine. He took my passport and asked me, "Do you know what's going on in your country, young man?" He thought maybe I had no idea what was happening.

I replied, "Yeah, I know, but it's a long story. I can't explain it to you, but I have to be back in Ukraine." He scanned my passport and returned it to me.

I took a picture of crossing the border back to Ukraine while I was thinking, *Are you sure, Alex? Are you sure? Because you will not be able to leave the country again.* I was at the point of no return trusting God.

Once I crossed the border, I saw those thousands of people close up. There were no markets or stores in that area where they could get food or water. They were cold. They were thirsty. They were hungry. Some of them were crying. They were broken and fearful. The Lord spoke to me that this was my ministry: serving the internally displaced and refugees in Ukraine.

My assistant from when I was starting out as a pastor, Serhei Kvasha, came with his mother to meet me at the border. They shared with me that they had spent 15 hours waiting at the checkpoint with about 12 of their family members, only to be denied passage. Since men were not allowed to leave the country, the women of Serhei's family decided they would not leave their husbands behind. They drove me back to Izmail.

For those couple of hours on our way back, I texted some people who were active in my church. I shared with them that the Lord had brought me back to Ukraine for ministry, and by that time I understood I was going to minister to the internally displaced and refugees. I texted them, "I'm going to do this ministry, and I would love for you to participate in it with me. If you want to join me in this venture, let's meet tomorrow morning in the church."

I had no idea if anyone would respond because I knew that people were panicking. It was chaos. Church members had the desire to leave the country, just like those people at the border did. Many people were looking for a chance to leave, maybe even by paying money under the table. I had no idea if anyone was going to show up to the meeting.

The next morning when I arrived at the church, 10 people were waiting for me. It was such a great inspiration for me because first of all, it was confirmation that this was what God wanted me to do. Second, it proved that He is faithful. He had said, "I'm going to provide and supply everything for the ministry," and He started supplying with the human resources needed to serve the refugees. I knew there wasn't much I could do on my own, but God provided a team of people who would help me run the ministry.

Together we determined the main needs we were able, at that moment, to meet for the people. I shared with them what I had seen on the border— that people were staying there 25 hours and were hungry and thirsty. I proposed, "Let's cook some food and hand out some snacks. We can collect heating boilers for the water and make hot drinks. Let's set up tables where people can stop by, and while they eat and drink, we can talk with them about Jesus and God's mercy and pray for them. Let's inspire them to find a church wherever they settle to help them start their new lives with Jesus."

We partnered with the Great Change Church to do this ministry of delivering food at the border and preaching. They are one of the new churches in our city with whom we are in a very good relationship. They also began running a refugee camp where they were hosting 200 internally displaced people. As much as I can, I also contribute to that ministry with funds I receive from the United States.

Our team arrived at the border in the evening, and we set up a table covered with snacks and hot drinks. I made an announcement to the people standing in line who were fleeing the country: "We're scared, just like you. We know what is going on in our country and why you want to leave. We're here to help. We know you're thirsty and hungry. We want to give you these snacks and drinks. This is free for you. Please come and help yourself."

I expected them to all come to the table because they had stayed in line for so many hours, but I was shocked to see that no one took a step out of the queue—not one person. I wondered, *What's going on?*

I made a second announcement, saying, "This isn't poisonous. We want to bless you, to help you. We want to pray for you."

A man who was standing in line with his wife and children called out to us, "We can't take a step out of this queue. If we step out to get these drinks and food from you, we'll immediately lose our spot in this line. I don't want to stay another eight or 10 hours here with my kids to get to the same spot."

So, we found out that the only option for us to help the people standing in line at the border was to bring the snacks and drinks to them. There we were able to pray for them, talk with them about God, inspire them, and comfort them as much as possible.

We were learning. It was a new situation for us. I remember I was about to give a snack to a small girl who was in line with her mom. I had almost handed it to her when her mom screamed and pleaded, "Please don't give it to her!"

I was curious. "But why? Why don't you want us to help your kids? You probably have been staying here for, I don't know, for many hours. I'm not sure how long she's been hungry. Why don't you want us to help your daughter?"

Her answer was heartbreaking: "Yes, my daughter is hungry. I know that. We've been standing here for 10 hours. But I also know if she eats this now, then in just a little while, she will need a bathroom. I'll have to leave this queue to find a place in this field for her to use the restroom, and we'll lose our spot in this line."

That was heartbreaking to hear and see, but I understood her choice. She preferred that her daughter stay hungry in order to leave the country as soon as possible because they were afraid. We helped those people who accepted our help and prayers. It was a great opportunity for us to be alive in the world. We said that we were helping because we were Christians.

About two days after our church's first trip to the border, the sound of a missile landing woke me up in the morning. I live on the fifth floor of a Soviet apartment building. The higher your apartment, the more you feel the ground shaking. I heard two missiles land. I had no idea if they had hit my city or somewhere outside of it, but it was scary. I found out later that the missiles had landed in a local military unit, which is about 24 kilometers (15 miles) from Izmail. I heard my neighbors talking in the hallway. They were saying, "Okay, let's pack our bags. It has started in our city. We have to leave."

Immediately, I got a lot of calls. People from the church who knew what we were doing and that we were helping internally displaced people started calling me and asking, "Are you providing transportation to the border?"

When I was coming back to my city after re-entering Ukraine, I found out about the transportation situation. People were coming to my city from all over Ukraine using regular transportation such as trains and buses, but once they got here they were stuck, because there was no public transportation to the border. The only option for them was a taxi. All the taxi drivers had the revelation that this was their time to prosper and doubled or tripled their fees. It's very shameful, but that's what happened. The hike in prices made taxis unaffordable for most people. That's when they began calling us asking for rides.

That day I got our church team together and said, "We still have the vans that we used years ago to deliver food and supplies to the east side of our country. Let's use those same vans now to provide free rides for people to get to the border."

We didn't even have to make an announcement; it was enough for me to respond to several phone calls and say that yes, we would supply transportation for people from our church every morning at 10:00. The word spread quickly. Every day people called me: "Are you still supplying transportation?" "Yes, we are. Please come to the church tomorrow at 10:00." We saw people gather in our church every morning at around 9:00.

My wife, Anastasia, who stayed in Romania, found out what the Romanian policies concerning Ukrainian refugees were: where they could stay and where they could get their food, medical support, and free SIM cards for voice and data. She found out how they could get from Romania to other countries in Europe. Anastasia passed along that basic but very important information to us, and we supplied it to the people who gathered at the church for a free ride. Then, the other ministers from our church and I were able to preach to them and lead some of them in the prayer of salvation. After that, we gave them a free ride to the border.

People couldn't afford a taxi ride, so they were very thankful. It was pleasing for me to think that those people who had lost so many things, who were broken, would have as their final memories of their country some people who extended hope and kindness to them. At the time when they had lost everything, and when taxi drivers wanted to charge them triple the price, there was a church of God with Christian people who advised them, prayed for them, inspired them, and gave them a free ride. We were even able to provide rides for people from the war zone, mainly women and children. Within the first month of the invasion, we gave free rides to 500 people.

This part of the ministry took teamwork on both sides of the border, with my wife meeting people in Romania and helping them find a place to stay. We did that for a month, and then the Red Cross and the local government finally took over that responsibility.

About the time when we were transitioning away from transporting people to the border, I received calls from some missions organizations and churches that wanted to partner with us in our ministry. I posted information on my Facebook page about my return to Ukraine and how our team was helping people, and I sent it to some other people personally.

Crossing the border back into Ukraine on February 26, 2022

The first volunteers to serve

People started reaching out to me by email and phone, saying, "Alex, we know what you are doing, and we want to help you. We want to provide things for you." It's interesting that I never asked for help—I had no time to do so. People started reaching out to me, however, just as the Lord had promised. He had said, "I'm going to supply and provide," and that's exactly what happened. We were able to do more and more. The ministry was growing.

Go Back

Preaching to people before giving them a ride to the border

Evacuating people to the border

CHAPTER 4

OPEN DOORS

My wife, our children, and my brother-in-law stayed in Romania for six weeks. Anastasia aided our ministry efforts by meeting people we helped evacuate on the other side of the border, counseling them, instructing them, and helping them get to the right place, along with other vital things of that nature. One month after the invasion, the Red Cross finally got involved and started to take over these responsibilities from us. Because of the size of their organization, they had many more resources and opportunities than we did and could help many more people. We realized that it was no longer necessary for us to continue with that ministry emphasis.

Because Anastasia was no longer meeting Ukrainian refugees on the Romanian side of the border, she moved with our two kids and her brother to the campus of the Baptist Theological Seminary in Bucharest, Romania. The seminary was gracious enough to allow Ukrainian refugees to stay on their campus for free, and even provided three meals a day.

It was a huge blessing for Anastasia and all the other Ukrainians staying there, but the situation wasn't ideal. To start with, there was a language barrier. Most people in Romania speak Italian, not English, because it is very similar to the Romanian language. Additionally, Romania had a policy preventing Ukrainian refugees' children from going to school. Also during that period of time, Anastasia couldn't work. My family's time living on that campus, as wonderful as it was for them to stay there, was quite boring because they had nothing to do.

Not long after my family arrived at the seminary, they found out that Canada had opened its borders to Ukrainians. Canada had waived visa fees and were issuing work permits to Ukrainian refugees as they got off planes in the airports. The Canadian government was saying, "Come to Canada. You can work and live here, and if you want, you can stay here forever." There is a large population of Ukrainians who live in Canada, and they wanted to help their countrymen who were fleeing the war zone.

My wife called me while I was working on transitioning to a different direction in our ministry, and she said, "What do you think of the kids and me moving to Canada?"

I dismissed the idea at first. "It's too far. When you are close by, you can come to Ukraine and we can at least see each other every once in a while, but I have no connections in Canada."

On the other hand, I had been traveling to the United States for years and had friends there. I thought perhaps some of them would agree to help us, but at that time the U.S. hadn't opened the doors for Ukrainians. The only way for Ukrainians to get to the U.S. was to go through Mexico, where there was a special procedure. We couldn't imagine my wife traveling with two kids across Mexico—where she had never been—to get to the border in Tijuana. It was too complicated. I also knew that at that time, it took some months for Ukrainians to get a work permit in the U.S., while Canada was much more flexible with its rules and policies for Ukrainians.

But again, I didn't know anyone in Canada, and that's what I told Anastasia: "I know a lot about the U.S., but I've never been to Canada. I have nobody there."

Still, she insisted, "I feel that the Lord wants us to go there."

I wasn't quite sure about that, so I responded, "If you feel that way, you'll have to look for a family who will host you because I don't know anyone there. We'll also have to think through some questions. Where in Canada will you go? What city and province? Let's say you research the top 10 best cities to live in Canada and you choose one of them. You arrive at the airport. What are you going to do from there? Are you going to take a taxi to a hotel? How long can you stay in the hotel? How are you going to find a job once you get there? Do we have enough money for this? I have no idea how we can make this work."

She said, "Okay. I'm going to pray about all that."

Now, part of my family moved to the United States five years ago. Anastasia contacted my brother Dan, who lives in Dallas, Texas. He's a videographer who works with different companies. She knew that he had gone to Canada for work a couple of years ago to make a video for a company there, so she reached out to him.

She asked, "Do you know of somebody in Canada who would agree to host a Ukrainian family—your relatives—for one or two months? It would just be until we get jobs and save enough money to rent a place of our own."

He said, "I can't promise anything, but I will try to find someone."

A couple of days later, there were some ministers who came to the seminary campus where my family was staying to talk with and pray for the Ukrainians there. That evening, there was a special time of prayer. Anastasia attended the prayer gathering with our children and told the ministers our situation.

She explained, "We want to go to Canada, but we don't know anyone there. Can we pray together for us to find a host family in Canada?"

They prayed, and not even one hour later, she and I both got an email from a couple we didn't know named Rosalee and Cecil Gordon. We found out they were from Calgary, Alberta.

The email said, "We know you're looking for a host family in Canada. Here's some information about our family and some pictures of us. Here are some pictures of our house. We want you to know that we are happy to help you. We have a basement unit, where you can stay as long as you need. We also have a second car that you might be able to use sometimes. You are welcome here. Please, fly to Calgary, and we'll meet you at the airport. We'll help you any way we can."

Anastasia called me immediately asking if I had seen the email. I said, "Yes, I've seen it, but I'm not sure about this. We don't know these people. It's so foreign to us, and I don't know if this is the best option."

All this was happening at the time when some friends of my church started supporting our ministry. I didn't want to keep anything secret from them and have them find out later that I had moved my family. I emailed them and was very open about our situation, telling them, "As you know, my family is in Romania. They have nothing to do there. They don't know the language. It looks like there is a possibility for them to fly to Canada because Canada has extended an open invitation to Ukrainian refugees. Recently, a Canadian family emailed us saying that they want to host my family. What do you think about this? I would really appreciate your opinion and advice."

All of them were in agreement. They replied, "Yes, if you have the chance, do that. Have your family move to Canada. We're for it." One of the people I contacted for advice was Dan Christman, the friend who called me on the very first day of the invasion to say that I should move my family to Romania. I texted him to share what we were thinking about doing.

He called me and said, "Alex, I wouldn't think longer than 10 seconds if I had a chance to move my family to Canada in your situation. I would do it. Please send me their passport information because I want to buy airline tickets for them."

Dan's offer was unexpected, but it was a great joy. However, I felt a little shy. I said, "That's very generous of you, but I would never ask you to do that. I just wanted to know your opinion about what we should do. Plus," I added, "it's not just my wife—it's also my two kids and my wife's brother. That's four people. I already researched the price for tickets, and I know it's going to cost a lot."

But he replied, "Alex, don't worry about it. Through all my travels I have gained a lot of frequent flyer miles, and I'm happy to purchase the tickets."

This whole situation was a great miracle testimony for our family. God was opening doors all around us for them to move to Canada: there was a family who contacted us saying they wanted to host our family, and Dan Christman wanted to buy the airline tickets. *Okay,* I thought, *it looks like God is trying to say something to me.* I acquiesced: "Okay, let's do it." Dan bought the tickets. We told the family in Calgary that we humbly and gratefully accepted their offer.

On April 15, 2022, my family flew from Romania to Calgary. The Gordons met them at the airport. They are great people, and they really took care of my family. The Gordons helped them acclimate to the new culture, climate, and rules—it was a completely new world for them.

Only God could have made my family's move to Canada possible. When I talked with the people in Izmail about my family, they thought that I had moved my family to the United States, but I told them I hadn't. The people in my city knew that my father, mother, and three of my siblings were living in the U.S. and that I had visited them there in the past. They reasonably assumed that I had moved my family to the U.S. and were surprised when I told them they were in Canada. The people I told would always ask, "Do you know anyone in Canada?"

I would reply, "No. I've never been to Canada, and I don't know anyone there, but my brother's friends are hosting my family now." That's what I was telling them.

In fact, when my father-in-law found out my

family had moved to Calgary, he told me jokingly, "I see you are a really picky person."

I said, "Picky? What do you mean?" Because, once again, I knew nothing at all about Canada.

He said, "You chose to move your family to the best city to live in Canada."

I didn't know what he was talking about: "What do you mean?"

Now *he* was confused. "I thought you picked the city."

"No. I never really researched it."

He said, "Google the best cities to live in the world, and you'll find that Calgary is in fourth or fifth place in some lists."

I was stunned. "Really?"

"Yes," he said.

That, to me, was the Lord. Even though I didn't know it, the Lord had found hosts for my family in one of the best cities in Canada. That was miraculous to me.

Because of what our ministry had done for the military in Ukraine with the help of Eckhard Baumann, which I will explain in greater detail in Chapter 5, the Odessa regional government, with the help of my friends, issued me a permit at the end of June 2022 that allowed me to travel out of Ukraine. It was very difficult to get that permission, but I told them, "For me to be able to continue this ministry, I have to travel to the United States, and I have to give reports and updates to the people who've been supporting us. Without that support, I may not be able to continue this ministry. I also need to see my family."

With that special traveling permit, I finally managed to go to Canada at the end of June 2022, after more than four months of being apart from my family. It was such a great blessing to be able to see them and to give thanks to the family who had hosted them.

My family was blessed in Canada. My brother-in-law got a job as an IT worker and my wife worked two part-time jobs, so they were able to rent an apartment after two months of staying with the Gordons. My family didn't want to be too much of a burden on their hosts. However, they did become friends with the Gordons, so the apartment they found was only a seven-minute drive from the Gordons' house so they could easily stay in touch.

When I visited Calgary, I wanted to give the Gordons my personal thanks. I assumed that my brother Dan was the key person who introduced us and asked them to host my family. On Sunday after church, I asked Rosalee if she could share with me the story of how she met my brother. "I'm curious: how did you become friends?"

She said, "Alex, I'll tell you something now. The day when I got an email from Dan asking me to host his family, all I knew about Dan was his first name. I didn't even know his last name."

I said, "What do you mean? I told the people in Ukraine that you were *friends* with Dan, and that because of your friendship, you agreed to host my family. Now you're telling me that the day he sent you an email, the only thing you knew about him was his first name?"

She said, "I think he figured I met him two years ago, but all I knew then was my company had hired this guy from the U.S. to record and edit a video for us. I was in the video that he worked on, so he knew my name and what I looked like. Somehow, he thought that he knew me because he knew what I looked like. He knew *my* name, but I never met him in person. I had never talked with him before the day he emailed me.

"But the reason why I agreed to host your family when he asked was this: The day before I received his email, I was sitting on the couch in my living room watching TV. There was news about Ukraine and all the devastation there. I felt so bad for your country. My heart went out to the Ukrainians suffering there, and I felt awful that there was nothing I could do to help them. It was like a grave in my heart. The following day, I got an email from your brother with a request to help his Ukrainian family. I immediately responded, 'Yes, I want to help,' and that's how your family came to live with us."

The timing was incredible. Rosalee reached out to us one hour after my wife prayed with the ministers to find a host family. All these things were put together like a puzzle in the miraculous picture of my family's transition from Romania to Canada. It was a miracle for me before, with the family that wanted to host my family and then with the airline tickets, but when I heard the rest of the story—that Rosalee never knew my brother before, that she just wanted to help Ukrainians because of what she had seen on the news, and that the *next day* she got my brother's email—it became such a marvelous picture for me of how great and good our God is.

What are the chances of all these pieces coming together so perfectly—my brother Dan from Dallas, my family from Romania, and Rosalee from Calgary watching the news? They're incredibly slim, but I think the chances are even less if we add the additional requirements that this family be a Christian family and leaders in their church. When my family

Go Back

arrived in Calgary, they were amazed to discover that their hosts met both those requirements, which makes this story even more special. God worked everything out perfectly so my family could live with nice people who welcomed them into their home and church. He opened every door, even when I thought moving my family to Canada could never work. Just like God promised, He provided everything my family needed.

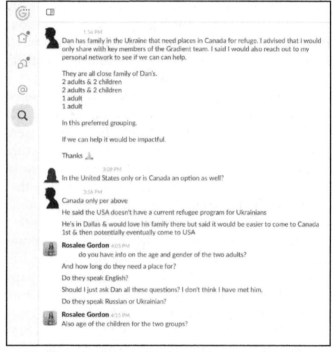

The discussion between Rosalee and her co-workers about hosting my family

Oleksandr Ilash

Rosalee Gordon meeting my family in the airport on April 15, 2022

My family arrived safely in Calgary
From left to right: my daughter, Lika; my wife, Anastasia; my brother-in-law, Nikita; my son, Joseph; and Rosalee Gordon

CHAPTER 5

ADAPTING TO CHANGING NEEDS

I have told the story of how God called me to return to Ukraine and minister to refugees there. Our initial focus was on the border—providing food, drinks, and transportation to people waiting to get out, while simultaneously preaching the gospel to them. As the government and other organizations took over that need, we transitioned to other areas of focus. But before I get into the specifics of our ministry, I think it's important to give an overview of the refugee situation in my area specifically and Ukraine in general. Keep in mind that by the time you read this, things may have changed.

Before the war hit the country, my city, Izmail, had a population of about 80,000 people. It's not a mega-city. Since the war began, we have gained an additional 50,000 people (as of May 2023) who were internally displaced. There are two categories of men who were permitted to flee the war zone and leave the country: the disabled and those who have three or more children.

Those who were able to leave the country have scattered all around the world, ending up in Europe, the U.S., Canada, and Australia. However, there are many more who have been internally displaced or who can't leave the country for whatever reason. According to statistics as I write, Ukraine has up to 12,000,000 people who are internally and externally displaced, out of a population of 40,000,000. That means the war has displaced one quarter of all the people in Ukraine.

Most men were required to stay in Ukraine, and many women decided to stay with their husbands rather than travel to another country with their children. Those people then want to be in the safest possible place within Ukraine, and that's the reason many of them have moved to border cities on the western side of my country, such as Izmail.

When we record who they are, we ask the refugees where they have come from and why they have left. Very often they respond, "My city doesn't exist any longer. It was burned to the ground." There are a number of cities in the east and south of Ukraine where there is no sense in trying to rebuild because everything is completely destroyed. Even if the war ceased tomorrow, these people would have nothing to go back to. They have lost everything—their houses, savings, and even family members.

The refugees are all different ages, but they all have one thing in common: they have to start over from scratch. That's why they make their way to our church. We help provide them with simple things such as clothing, mattresses, food, groceries, and medication. Many of them are unable to find a job because the economy is poor as a result of the war. They depend on ministries and churches such as ours to provide for their basic needs.

There are two main aspects of our current ministry: the refugee camp and the church. We provide aid to the internally displaced people who stay in a nearby refugee camp by helping them find jobs, providing them with a place to stay, and giving them food every day. The second part of our ministry is in our church building, where we have a team of volunteers serving people who come into our church five days a week. They start showing up at 1:00 p.m., and our food and supply distribution lasts until 7:00 p.m.

We serve up to 350 people each day for five days a week. We give out bags of groceries, and once a month we also supply diapers and medication. The refugee camp we help with is 40 kilometers (25 miles) from the city and houses about 200 people, 50 of which are children. The camp is run by Great Change Church, and we help provide them with supplies.

When the war began, Great Change Church rented a place to help the refugees, but nobody thought this war would last as long as it has. They hosted those refugees at a nice, rented facility for about five months. Our church was helping them with finances, groceries, and supplies, but then after those five months, the owner increased the rent. Great Change Church couldn't afford to keep renting it, so they bought a few old camping units that were on sale and began to renovate them with the help of different donors, including our church.

The new camp is set up so people can reside

there even during cold winter days. At the time of this writing, it houses 200 people, but we hope to help renovate another two buildings to make room for an additional 100 people. The people who come to the camp can stay there up to three months while they look for jobs and places to rent in the suburbs. Every morning we hold devotions for them because people there are stressed and in shock. They have seen death. They are emotionally broken, and they are in very distressed mental conditions.

For the first two weeks after they arrive, we don't bother them. We supply them with food and a safe place to stay, and that's it. Then, after two weeks, our ministers start working with them, praying for them, and counseling them. A few weeks after that, we help them look for jobs and a more permanent place to stay. The refugee camp ministry is not only about giving people food and shelter, but also about coming alongside them as they start their new lives in a new place.

The main focus of our ministry is the city of Izmail, where our church is located. People start arriving at our church every day at 1:00 p.m., and we invite them into the sanctuary. There we pray for them and preach to them, leading some of them in the prayer of repentance. After that, we do the actual distribution of food. Most often we put what we have on a long table, and people can take what they need. We do this for about 1,000 people per week, or about 5,000 per month. We also have a van that delivers food and supplies to the sick and elderly—approximately 50 homes per week, or about 200 addresses per month. Other churches do a similar food distribution outreach but are focused mainly on the villages around Izmail. We distribute food in the villages just once each week because our center of attention is in the city.

There are two ways we acquire supplies. I share what we are doing with churches and missions, and some of them provide a shipping container of supplies from time to time. We buy the rest of the things that people need. Some of the food we buy is produced in Ukraine or our neighboring country, Romania. To buy there, we cross the border, deliver it to our storage facility, and distribute it to people. What we distribute comes from people who send us resources and supplies that we are able to purchase. We are grateful for all our donors who have made this ministry possible. God has used them to keep His promise to provide all we would need.

We distribute food and supplies, but most importantly, we preach the gospel to the people we serve. Most of the adults were born and raised under Communism, which means that they never heard the truth about the gospel or Jesus. If they claim to be Christians, they are often connected with the Russian Orthodox Church, which can be more tradition-focused, and sometimes the people lack a personal relationship with God, even though they know about Him, His Holy Spirit, and Jesus. We are using this terrible time to preach the gospel to some of them for the very first time.

Because the war has lasted for so long, the needs we were having to meet have changed. For example, in the first month of the war, we helped people with transportation, evacuating them from the war zone to the border so they could get to a safe place in Europe. Police departments, recruiting offices, and other military units were not prepared and did not even have supplies to cook food for the influx of conscripts and volunteers. So, for the first two months, our ministry cooked and delivered food every day for 200 police and territorial defense soldiers. The government was eventually able to take on that responsibility.

Our train station ministry is another example of how we have adapted to changing needs. We found out early on that people came to Izmail by train every morning on the way to the border. The train pulled into the station at 4:45 a.m., and someone recommended that it was another opportunity for ministry: "Those people who come on the train are thirsty and hungry. It would be nice if we could meet them with some snacks and drinks."

When I heard that, I said, "This is a great opportunity for us to preach to those people and be a light to them."

The other church volunteers agreed, and so every morning at 4:45, we were at the train station. We brought bottled water, snacks, cookies, and small New Testaments donated by the Gideons. At least 300 people arrived every day. They had to pass through the main hall at the railway station, so that's where we met them with those supplies. They did not expect our generosity and were quite appreciative of that small gesture. We were able to preach to them and pray for their salvation.

We ran the ministry at the railway station for about 45 days. Within that time period, I didn't see any other pastors there from other churches. I did, however, see a Muslim businessman who was doing the same thing we were—distributing cookies and other snacks. He was a rich businessman who was moved with compassion. He would urge the people to heed the words of a Christian pastor, saying that I had something important to tell them.

It was phenomenal—Christian pastors and ministers and a Muslim businessman were working together to help and provide supplies to people in need. We did the train station ministry until Russia launched a missile that struck a large bridge across the lake. I will tell you the story about the bridge later because it is part of my testimony. That bridge had a railway that ran from Odessa to Izmail, so when the bridge was destroyed, the train simply stopped coming to Izmail. Till the very last day, we were carrying out that ministry at 4:45 a.m.

My daily schedule was waking up at 4:00 a.m. to be at the railway station by 4:45, then returning to the church to prepare for the food distribution so we could deliver food to the military and refugees. At the end of the day, I had to send reports, pictures, and videos to our donors. At one point, I sent reports every night—updates about Ukraine and how far the Russian soldiers had invaded, what damage had been done, and how we were able to help and supply people.

Today I write fewer reports because I am so busy, but I still want our donors to know how vital their support is and will continue to be. But, just as the Lord said, He supplied and provided everything. People and organizations started reaching out to us. Various missions, churches, and organizations joined the aid efforts, including the Pentecostal Assemblies of the World (PAW), Apostolic World Christian Fellowship, Apostolic Ministers Alliance (AMA), and Feed the Hungry.

As I explained in Chapter 3, we had determined the direction of the ministry by the beginning of March 2022. Bishop Michael D. Franklin, who had previously called to offer the PAW's help when my family was evacuating to Romania, reached out to me only a few days after I had returned to Ukraine. I was invited to participate in a video call with all the bishops, who were having a board meeting in Tampa. I shared with them what was going on in my country and the ways our team was ministering to people here. They prayed for me virtually—for us and for our ministry—and made the decision to help and support us.

Bishop Michael D. Franklin and Presiding Bishop Theodore Brooks also asked to do a livestreamed interview with me on the PAW's Facebook page. They wanted me to share about what was going on in Ukraine as a part of a fundraiser for PAW churches to support our ministry's efforts. Presiding Bishop Theodore Brooks interviewed me on Facebook Live three times. That was a great honor. He paid attention to Ukraine's plight and was moved with compassion. He did his best to inform people about what was going on here in Ukraine and inspired them to give to our ministry, and the result was amazing.

In the very beginning of January 2023, Bishop Michael D. Franklin and Bishop Glenn Brady from Kansas City, Kansas, came to Ukraine for a few days as official delegates from the PAW to help us in our ministry. It was a very productive trip. The bishops preached a Christmas message in our church to internally displaced people and prayed the prayer of repentance with many. They also prayed for soldiers and helped distribute food to 500 people in Komyshivka village.

Bishops Franklin and Brady brought donated gifts to give to the children of internally displaced families. The bishops also took part in our Christmas charity and organized a banquet for widows and elderly people. The Christmas banquet was in a restaurant that fit a good number of people. They preached the gospel and helped with multiple aspects of our ministry, including outstanding service to the youth, while they were here. We were very grateful and blessed to not only receive financial support from the PAW, but also to have their representatives come and physically serve alongside us. They were able to see the need with their own eyes and confirm that this ministry is needed these days.

During the publishing process for this book, I attended the international PAW convention at the end of July 2023 to represent Ukraine and to give thanks to the PAW for all their support. I was able to speak on stage about our ministry, present a very special Ukrainian flag to Presiding Bishop Theodore Brooks, and to again thank the PAW for their contributions to our ministry in Ukraine.

My good friends Pastors Michael and Tami Keller from Grand Rapids, Michigan, who visited us in Ukraine a few years ago as well, reached out to me and said that their church's alliance wanted to help us financially. They did a fundraiser in their church and throughout the AMA network. Additionally, their daughter, Erica, connected with a few small businesses that sold some items to help financially support our ministry in Ukraine. The PAW and the AMA were by no means the only supporters of our ministry, but I wanted to especially recognize their contributions and dedication to helping internally displaced people in Ukraine.

A friend of mine, Eckhard Baumann, who is the founder and CEO of Straßenkinder ministry in Berlin, Germany, also reached out to me. Straßenkinder is an NGO for homeless children and is very well supported in Germany. My family has been friends with him for a decade. We never talked about any kind of support; he was just a good friend of mine who would visit us, and I would visit him in Germany.

A couple of weeks after the war began, Eckhard saw some of the updates I posted on what our church was doing, and he called me and said, "Alex, I started supporting Ukrainian ministers and churches who do these kinds of humanitarian efforts. I would love to support what you're doing as well."

He said he specifically wanted to help the Ukrainian army, especially Christian Ukrainian soldiers. "I'll help with humanitarian efforts," he said, "but I'm especially interested if you have the opportunity to help Ukrainian soldiers."

For about the first six months of the war, the military's need for supplies was extensive, because they were not prepared for the large numbers of young men who were joining the army and territorial defense units. They had no supplies—no body armor, no special winter shoes, nothing. We were getting a lot of calls from members of our church and other local churches asking if we were providing supplies to soldiers.

Eckhard stepped up. We had no resources to help in this area, but he began sending either funds for us to buy supplies or actual supplies from Germany that he purchased there and then shipped to us. We were able, together with our humanitarian efforts, to cook for and feed people who needed it. We were also able to help our Ukrainian brothers who went to the front line or to checkpoints throughout the city.

With Eckhard's help, we supplied body armor, tourniquets, and bandages to soldiers. We committed to providing food for two months to a local military unit comprised of 200 soldiers. We also delivered food to patrols, the police station, and to checkpoints around the city. The Lord provided through this man, even though I never asked him for support. He just called me and said, "I want to help you."

Because of Eckhard's support, we were able to pursue this new avenue of ministering to soldiers in addition to our main ministry of feeding, evacuating, and distributing supplies to refugees. The national and local governments appreciated the work we were doing to help the armed forces. It elevated the authority of the church. We're pro-Ukraine—we're not only taking care of civilians, but we also want our country to get a victory. That's why we were helping our soldiers. This was also a great opportunity to preach to the soldiers. With the way the rotations worked, they could be in a local military unit at first, but in two weeks they could be sent to the front line. We were so thankful to get the chance to talk with them about Jesus and to lead some of them in the prayer of repentance, because many of them, unfortunately, die on the front line.

We carried out the ministry to the military for the first few months of the war, concurrently with the train station ministry. Once the trains stopped coming, we spent the next several months establishing a daily food distribution ministry at our church, as described earlier in this chapter. Everything was going well. We were able to use what we had and what our donors were supplying to help the refugees who were coming to our church, but we found out there were certain groups of people who could not get to the church because they were disabled, sick, or elderly. Some of them couldn't move more than 50 meters (about 160 feet) a day. These non-mobile refugees were staying in their relatives' apartments, houses, or rental places, and they or their friends would call us saying, "Would you be able to deliver food to those people? Would you be able to deliver diapers to those old people? Would you be able to deliver some medication to those people?"

We had no additional transportation to do that. I shared this with Eckhard, and he purchased a van for us in Germany and had it delivered to us at the end of May 2022. It wasn't brand new, but it was in very good condition.

We got another nice van with the help of Greater Grace Temple in Detroit, Michigan, where my new friend Bishop Charles H. Ellis III is a pastor. After a special video call that we had on one of those scary days in March 2022, we got to know each other, and Bishop Ellis was filled with compassion for the people of Ukraine and our ministry here. He has done outstanding work, inspiring his people to give and keeping them updated about our ministry. As a result of that divine connection, our ministry received a second van and financial support for our efforts. That was an unexpected but timely blessing for our ministry. Now we use those two vans for food delivery to the surrounding villages and the addresses of the disabled, sick, and elderly. We can also use them to transport people when we have to.

We identified several people from our team to oversee this new ministry direction. They fielded the calls, and then put together a list of people's names and addresses who wanted us to come and help them. Five other people from our team started driving around the city and the villages three times a week in the vans that were donated to us, delivering food and talking with people face-to-face. They talked with them about Jesus and prayed with them. When we meet with people in our sanctuary, it is not usually one-on-one, but our mobile team was able to more effectively minister to the people's individual needs.

Very often we visited people who were living on an upper floor of their building and never came out of their apartment. They couldn't walk, which is why they had to stay there. Some of them were alone and had no one to care for them because their relatives had left the country. We gave them food and other necessities, but we also gave them hope and encouragement.

We often comforted people by saying, "War is horrible, and we're all concerned and confused. We have no idea why this has happened to our country, but the fact is that we have come to your house now in the name of Lord to show you that God knows where you are, no matter what is happening in our country. God still cares. God still loves you, and that's why we're here. That's why we do what we do—because Jesus loves you." Because of all the calls we received, our church adapted its ministry to be in a position to help the people stuck in that situation and preach the gospel to them.

Beginning in April 2023, we started delivering food and groceries to the front line, to the villages that were hurt and damaged by missiles. One of our new directions is to do these trips to front line areas at least once a month, providing for people there and preaching to them. For example, in June 2023 our team traveled to Kherson and its suburb villages, which flooded after the Russians exploded a water dam there. Thousands of houses were underwater. When the water receded, the people who lived there had to start over with nothing. We delivered to them not just hope and the gospel, but also necessities such as beds and mattresses, hygiene items, clothes, electrical generators, and groceries. Our practical approach to ministry opened people's hearts to Jesus—in Kherson I prayed the salvation prayer with 200 people.

In summary, the needs are always changing. In the beginning, our main concern was evacuating people. As the need for transportation to the border diminished, the need at the train station in the mornings grew. When a Russian missile landed on the bridge and destroyed the railway and the train stopped coming to our city, we found other needs, like delivering food to the elderly or to the military.

We transitioned again as local governments were able to organize and prepare. Our main efforts then were with the food and supplies that we were giving to people in our church, which we do to this day. As of this writing, we are able to do a grocery distribution four times a week in our church, one day away in the villages, and also on Sunday after church, providing food for 250 to 350 people per day.

Within a year after I crossed the border back into Ukraine, we have been able to provide 50,000 grocery bags to the same number of people. By the end of July 2023, we will have given away 70,000 grocery bags. We have experienced the blessing and power of obedience. When God called me to go back to Ukraine, I had no idea what the ministry would be—I was stepping into the unknown. Now I see what it has become, but I also know there will be more changes as the needs arise. While all the details of the ministry have changed, the mission has not: to share the love of Jesus by helping the internally displaced in my country.

Christmas message at our church by Bishop Michael D. Franklin and 10 saved souls!

From left to right: Bishop Glenn Brady, me, and Bishop Michael D. Franklin distribute food to 500 people in Komyshivka village, Ukraine, on January 7, 2022

Bishop Michael D. Franklin and Bishop Glenn Brady preach the gospel to Ukrainian soldiers on January 7, 2022

Bishop Michael D. Franklin and Bishop Glenn Brady give food supplies to internally displaced people in Izmail, Ukraine, on January 8, 2022

CHAPTER 6

GREEN CARD

Before I go on with stories about our ministry, I think it's important to provide you with some background information about my family and the way God has worked in our lives since long before the war. My parents and some of my siblings moved to the U.S. in 2018, and the story of how they got there is a powerful testament to God's faithfulness and perfect plan for our lives.

Years ago, I was traveling with my father—whose name is also Alex—to the U.S. to raise funds for our ministry of delivering food and supplies after the first Russian invasion. We had connections to some churches. We had our U.S. visas. My father never planned or had the desire to move to the U.S. because he had a ministry in Ukraine. He felt good about his life there and had all he needed.

While we were on this fundraising trip in the U.S., my father got a call from a friend of his named

Steve, who lived in Sacramento, California. Steve asked him, "Pastor Alex, why don't you fill out the application for the green card lottery?"

My father said, "Why would I do that? I have my visa to travel to the United States. I never plan to move there. Why do I need to do that?"

Steve responded, "I was praying today, and God spoke to me that if you apply this year for a green card, you'll win it."

After the phone call, Dad said to me, "That was very brave of him to speak that way, but I'm not interested."

I had experience with the green card lottery because for many years I had filled out the application form for my family and me. Many Americans have never heard of the green card lottery, but it's a big deal in Ukraine because people want to move to the U.S.

The system works as follows: The window to fill out the forms opens in October and closes a month later. People from all around the world, excluding some Muslim countries, can apply, but there are only 50,000 green cards per year that are made available for the whole world. Every country has its own annual quota for green cards. Ukraine usually gets about 2,000 or 2,500 green cards for its population of 40,000,000. Of course, not everyone applies, but many millions, especially young people, do apply because they want to move to the U.S. for a better life.

I knew so many people, even from our church, who applied for green cards year after year, and they were never selected. I was told that the chance of winning a green card is less than 0.0001%.

But Steve had said, "Pastor, I heard it from God: if you apply for a green card, you will win it this time." Even though my father had said he was not interested, Scripture says that sometimes we have to test the spirits to see if they are from God. Therefore, my father said to me, "Since Steve said I would win it this time, then I want you to fill out a form in my name. Let's test it to see if that word is from God."

So I filled out the form for him. That same year, I filled out the form for 20 people total from my church and family. U.S. Citizenship and Immigration Services take six months to work with all that data, and then they post the results in May.

During that month, Dad and I were at a conference in Louisville, Kentucky. After the morning session, we went to the hotel to take a nap. It was May 6 to be exact, which was the day I was eligible to review the results of the lottery for the people for whom I had applied.

I began checking the results for each person. I checked it for my wife: *You have not been selected.* I checked it for myself: *You have not been selected.* I checked it for my mom: *You have not been selected.* For all 20 people, the results said, *You have not been selected.*

I checked my father's last, and it said, *Congratulations, you have been selected.*

My father was lying on the bed in our hotel room, when I stood up and said, "Dad, you will not believe this. You may think I'm kidding, but I'm not. I'm serious. You won a green card."

He said, "What? I can't believe it!"

I said, "Yes, out of all our people who applied, you are the only winner."

However, there is another step to the process. Just because Dad was selected didn't guarantee that he would be able to move to the U.S., because they then check out the applicant's background. The applicant has to pass a medical test and go through an interview in the U.S. Embassy. Then the officer makes the final decision as to whether the applicant is qualified to enter the country. We went home to continue the process.

The green card lottery policy states that a winner can take with him his spouse and their children who are under the age of 21. Our family has six children. I see God's miraculous planning in this story because three of those six children were under the age of 21 and were eligible to go with him to the U.S. They were not married. The three children who were above the age of 21 were already married, so there was no issue.

The three eligible children were happy, but Mom and Dad were trembling. They were in their 50s, so they were not ready to start their lives from zero, especially when they had a church and a successful ministry. Dad was adamant that he would not go, and that created some tension in the family. My siblings reminded my parents that some people were paying big money to move their kids to the U.S., and here was Dad with a chance to go for free! They felt it would be a big mistake for him to turn it down, and it would seem like he did not want a better life for his children. However, Dad would not be moved—he was staying in Ukraine.

Then one day, he did something crazy. He went up on stage in the church and spoke to the congregation: "You all know I won a green card, and I know a lot of you wanted to get the same chance. I know if you had won the lottery, you wouldn't hesitate. You would move your family to the U.S. immediately. But I don't want to do that. There is now a division in my family over this issue because my children really want to go. Here is where I stand: I'm not going to go unless someone who doesn't know this situation—who doesn't know what happened in my life—will come to our church and speak to me that God wants to move me to the U.S."

When he said that, I was sitting in the front pew and thought, *Come on, that's not going to happen. That's it. That's the end of the story.* I was positive about that, but if God has a plan, He knows how to accomplish it.

Just two weeks after Dad's declaration on the stage, a minister from Chicago came for a scheduled visit to our church to preach at a revival service. We held a normal service in the morning, but in the evening, the American pastor said he felt that God was going to use him in prophetic ministry to speak to people. I was the one who was interpreting for him, and he prophesied to many people in our church. He didn't know them, but I did, and I knew their life situations. When he prophesied to them, I saw that what he said was right on target, so that was confirmation for me that God really was using him.

Then in the middle of the service, he stopped the worship team, turned to my father who was in the front row, and said, "Pastor Alex, I don't know what it means. I don't know why I am saying this now, but I feel strongly that God wants me to tell you that you must prepare your leadership team and church board because you aren't going to be here much longer. God is going to move you out of this city, out of this country, and you have to prepare your church. I don't know why, but I see you in an American church ministering to people there."

This pastor from Chicago had no idea of what my father had said two weeks prior. As I was interpreting this for our people, I was thinking, *Wow, they will either believe, or they will think that we got into some agreement with this guy to speak these things.* I could see Dad was shocked.

The next day we drove the visiting pastor to the airport in Odessa. My father said, "Alex, do you think we should tell him the whole story?"

I said, "Yes, because he just confirmed to you that this is from God. And yes, he has to know the rest of the story."

We told him the whole story, and he rejoiced: "Wow! Now I see the whole picture. Yesterday I was hesitant to say to your congregation that you were going to leave and that I saw you in an American church. But at the same time, I felt strongly that God wanted me to say this, and now I understand why."

After that confirmation, Dad started the process of filling out the paperwork and going through all the procedures. They say another 25 to 30% of people who win a green card become ineligible because they don't complete the process, but with my family, every step was easy. They did the final interview, got approval, and then moved to Dallas, Texas, in 2018. Pastor George Hancock hosted them and helped them get settled and start their new life. He also used to visit us in Ukraine, and he knew the story of all these confirmations.

My family stayed in Texas for a few years, and then Dad decided to move to Florida with Mom and my younger brother. My sister had gotten married in Texas, so she and my second brother stayed in Dallas. As of this writing, part of my family is in North Port, Florida, near Sarasota, and part of my family is in Dallas.

Dad was the founder and pastor of the Well of Living Water Church in Ukraine, so after he left, many of our members proposed that I take over the church. However, I was involved in building a youth center, and all my attention was there. I did pray to God for guidance on the matter, and often I would say, "Lord, I want to be in Your will. I want to be where You want me to be. If You tell me to leave Ukraine and go to the poorest tribe in Africa and live there for the rest of my life, if it's clear that it's from You, I'll do it. But I don't want to do something if I'm not sure that it's from You."

I had seen that pastoral ministry is full of challenges, and I didn't want that to be the reason I would not accept the role. At the end of the day, I didn't hear God say to do so, and that's why I didn't take the position of senior pastor. I did agree to be a second pastor in the church, while a deacon who was with my father for many years took the position of senior pastor. Today we have a good relationship, and we run the church together. He regularly asks my opinion on matters, and we trust each other. He does more of the internal ministry to church members, while I am more involved with ministries to the youth and people outside of the church. I am also involved in raising funds, but I do preach once or twice a month on Sundays.

Before the war, we had about 250 people attend church on Sundays. With the war, we lost some of the people in our congregation who were scared, and they scattered to other places. We completely understand why that has happened. Yet, because of the people who have fled to our city, and because of our ministry supplying food, the numbers in our church have actually increased.

CHAPTER 7

PRESERVATION

In the first days of the war, missiles landed about 50 kilometers (30 miles) from Izmail. The Russians targeted a military base there, which was part of our country's defense system. People got nervous and started leaving as fast as they could. Since then, the closest missiles we have heard have been about 160 kilometers (100 miles) away.

Even though our area is relatively safe, I have been in several situations in which the Lord has thankfully preserved me. In one close call, the World Food Programme (WFP), an organization that had partnered with our ministry to help provide food to refugees, wanted to broker an agreement to unblock the seaports of Odessa. Right before Ukrainian Easter, David Beasley, executive director of the WFP, came to Ukraine, and I was privileged to work together with him and some high-ranking Christian politicians in my country. David and his team had to enter

Ukraine through Moldova, which is not far from me. My friend Veniamin Unguryan, a congressman in the Odessa parliament and a Christian leader, and I were asked to help.

We organized meetings for David Beasley and his team with the government, the mayor, and the governor in Odessa because they wanted to record videos at the seaports that were blocked. The WFP representatives told us that they knew Ukraine was the breadbasket for Europe, Asia, and Africa. David Beasley said that the WFP supplies food every year to 120 million people and that half of their supplies, which includes wheat, comes from Ukraine. The blocked Ukrainian seaports threatened to plunge Asian and African countries into a famine.

The WFP's mission was to record videos at the seaports and to push the process of negotiations with Russia in order to unblock Odessa's seaports and create a safe corridor for the shipment of grains. My friend Veniamin and I helped the WFP representatives by driving them where they needed to go and making the appointments with our local officials and governments. I spent that week in Odessa—which is 240 kilometers (150 miles) from Izmail—and most of us were in one residential apartment area. Veniamin and I wanted to get back to Izmail to be with the church for the Easter celebration weekend, but the WFP delegation stayed in Odessa in a hotel.

Just one hour after we left that apartment area, a Russian missile landed there, and some local people were killed and injured. Because of the prayers of saints all over the world, the Lord protected us. We had spent almost a week in that area, and not one hour after we left, a missile landed there. My life was spared. The next day was the start of Easter weekend, so our church spent the next few days celebrating Easter and praying for Ukraine.

Veniamin and I went back to Odessa on Monday and Tuesday to help carry out the WFP's mission there. On Tuesday, we had to be back in Izmail. There are two interstate highways to my city from Odessa. We were positive that we were going to take the highway that had a large bridge across the lake with railways and cars. That was the bridge trains crossed to get from Odessa to the train station in Izmail where we went to minister each morning. For some reason, at the very last moment, we changed our minds and took the other highway.

Thirty minutes after that decision, we got calls and notifications on our phones. The bridge on the other highway, the one we would have taken, had been destroyed by Russian missiles. Immediately we started calculating the time, mileage, distance, and speed at which we were driving, trying to figure out where we would have been if we had taken that interstate. If we had taken that route, we would have been on the bridge or really close to the bridge when it was destroyed. I believe the power of the prayers of people around the world changed our minds to take the other way. That's why I'm still alive and can write this book. Those two explosions that could have hurt or killed me—at the residential apartment and the bridge—happened in the span of four days.

Near the end of April 2022, there were some U.S. congressional representatives and senators who were invited to Ukraine by Pavel Unguryan. He's a Christian, has served several terms in parliament, and is currently the coordinator of the Ukrainian–American partnership platform. At that time, U.S.

leaders, including members of Congress, were not eligible to visit Ukraine—it was restricted for them by
the U.S. government. Those representatives made the
trip as private citizens, tourists traveling at their own
risk, without any bodyguards. It was dangerous for all
of us to go to Kyiv because, even though the Russians
had already been pushed back, they had left a lot of
mines behind. The areas we visited hadn't been completely demined yet, so there was a risk.

We gave the congresspeople a tour of Bucha,
Borodyanka, and other suburban areas around the
capital. We wanted them to see what had happened
when our army had pushed the Russians back from
Kyiv. We felt it was important that the world see all the
atrocities the Russian soldiers had committed against
our people: the killing, the torture of defenseless people, and the executions. We brought those members
of Congress to the areas where those horrible things
had happened, so they would know that it was not
Ukrainian propaganda. The reports they had heard
were true.

This was an emotional trip for all of us because we witnessed the exhumation of some of the
victims who had been dead for a few months. We saw
the atrocities with our own eyes, along with destroyed
bridges, buildings, apartments, and government buildings. We also talked firsthand with the victims of the
invasion.

After the U.S. representatives saw all of that
with their own eyes, they went back to their country
and urged Congress to help Ukraine. My president
had been pleading with all the world's governments
to provide us with weapons, but they were very slow
in making the decision to do so. That trip helped
speed up the process because the visitors had seen the

destruction and talked to the people, and thus their word carried weight and was influential. The U.S. government passed a lend–lease agreement soon after.

In addition to the broader influence of the trip, I was personally impacted by what I had seen. Izmail hadn't been bombed; those atrocities that had happened in Kyiv hadn't occurred here. In a sense, the war had been far away from us. But going to Kyiv, seeing all that with my own eyes, and talking with people definitely left a mark on my life.

Despite a few close brushes with death during my travels throughout Ukraine, my city of Izmail was reasonably safe because of its geographical position next to the Danube River. The Danube acts as the border to Romania, which is a member of NATO. I think the only reason why Putin and his army are not bombing the western border cities like Izmail is because the missiles might accidentally land in Romania. That would put Russia in direct conflict with NATO.

That being said, I have heard a Russian politician publicly express the desire to take Odessa and go on to Izmail. He mentioned my city by name. They want to capture it, but they would have to do so with soldiers. That is their long-term goal, but so far they can only do destruction with their missiles. Wherever Russian soldiers have been pushed back by the Ukrainian army, those cities and areas are being bombed mercilessly; but as of this writing, my city has been spared. Some people may say this is a blessing— that we are safe and everything is fine. They may be right. But at the same time, because of our convenient geographical position, our challenge is caring for an influx of 50,000 internally displaced people.

Every time a city is bombed, we know another

wave of people will come to Izmail looking for a safe place to stay. Families who might have initially stayed where they were because their city hadn't yet been bombed often change their minds after they see another death, another apartment building being destroyed right next to them. At that point, they want to save their lives, so they move to Izmail. As of May 2023, we have 50,000 refugees in our area, and I assume that by the time you read this book, we're going to get another couple thousand more. It's a huge challenge to see those people, to help them, and to provide for them, because the need is so large.

The winter of 2022–23 was a difficult one. Putin's plan was to knock out Ukraine's power grid so we wouldn't have any heat. Russian propaganda during the summer of 2022 and into the fall talked a lot about the coming winter and how the Ukrainians would have to cope with the cold. The Russians were targeting the critical infrastructure of our country with their missiles. They destroyed around 50% of electrical and heating plants, so there really was a threat that many people would freeze to death.

But God had mercy on the Ukrainian people this past winter. Through prayers, and because our Lord is the Lord of justice and He knows the situation, the winter was unusually warm. Some areas in my country had snow and negative temperatures, but on average this winter was much, much warmer than it usually is.

Even in my area, we had many people who had a problem with heating their houses, but with the help of our friends and partners, we were able to buy and distribute enough coal, firewood, and fuel briquettes to heat many homes. Our top priority while distributing the supplies was to women with children.

We wanted to make sure their kids were sleeping in a warm house and not freezing to death. The Lord not only provided us with the financial resources to purchase and distribute fuel so people could heat their homes, but He also helped us by sending an unusually warm winter. The Russian propagandists were disappointed because their plan had failed.

We have so many more testimonies of how the Lord showed Himself strong in the midst of tragedy. Even in our war-torn country, His name is being glorified. The church has become, like Jesus said, a city on a hill, a beacon of light to the world. We have seen a lot of miracles that have proven the power of prayer.

Another such miracle is the story of Odessa and an unusual storm. In mid-March 2022, about three weeks after Russia invaded, we heard that Russian vessels were being sent from Crimea to Odessa across the Black Sea. Their plan was to get as close as they could to the seashore, then put their Marines on smaller ships to get to the shore and conquer Odessa. Odessa is a very important geographical point for Ukraine. It has three major ports, which ship wheat and grains all over the world. Ukraine is famous as being the breadbasket for Europe. The economy of our country depends on Odessa, which is the reason Putin wanted to conquer it.

Our military was not prepared at that time to repel a Russian assault on Odessa. They told us that the water was not mined, there was no defense on the seashore, and nothing else was in place. It was a hopeless situation. The question wasn't *if* the Russians would take Odessa but *when*. Then someone mentioned the only thing that could stop the Russian army was some kind of storm on the Black Sea. If the storm was big enough, the smaller ships wouldn't be able to get close to the seashore. When the church heard about this one hope, Christians all across Ukraine started earnestly praying for such a storm.

Typically, the month of March is the time when the sea is calm in our area. It's when parents take their children and couples go to the seashore to enjoy the sea breeze, pretty view, and nice weather. For there to be a storm in March would require a miracle, but we were united. We prayed for Odessa, for the region, and for a storm.

God answered our prayers and preserved us. Miraculously, God sent three weeks of non-stop storms on the Black Sea. You can Google pictures of the March 2022 storm in Odessa to see what I mean. The storm gave us time to prepare, so our soldiers could mine the water and put all the defense systems in place to protect Odessa. During those three weeks, the Russian military ships were running out of water, food, and provisions, and they had to turn back to

Escorting the WFP delegation to Odessa

The apartment complex in Odessa that was hit with a missile not long after I left

Crimea. As of this writing, though missiles are being launched at it, Odessa has never been occupied by Russian soldiers. That did not happen because of smart generals or brave soldiers in Ukraine, but through the prayer of the church. Everyone knows it was a miracle.

Bucha

Borodyanka

Devastation in the suburbs of Kyiv

March 2022 storm in Odessa

CHAPTER 8

PERSONAL IMPACT

I mentioned in the previous chapter that there are many testimonies of what God has done during this time of war, and in this chapter, I want to share some stories of how God is using our ministry to impact individuals' lives.

Part of our current ministry consists of delivering food and various supplies to those who are elderly, disabled, or sick. They call us to request our support and help, and then people from our church use a van to make the deliveries and share the gospel with them.

One day, I was involved in the food delivery. I had a list of people who had called us. We visited one woman who gave us another address. She said, "I'm not sure, but maybe someone needs your help there."

I took the paper on which she had written the address, but I thought, *I'm not going to go there because I already have a list of people who are waiting for me. I don't*

77

really have time to drive somewhere just to check if someone needs my help there.

When I thought that, I heard the same voice inside that I had heard during the conference in Kyiv or while I was praying in my secret room in Romania. The voice said, "Alex, you want to go there, and you want to see what's going on."

I decided, *Okay, Lord, if this is You, if You want me to go there, I will be obedient. I don't know if anyone needs my help there, but if You want me to go there, I will.*

We arrived at the address, which was a small, private home. When I knocked, a girl who was maybe 13 years old opened the door. I introduced myself, asked if there were any adults in the house, and if I could come in. She invited me in, and I went to the living room along with the other volunteers who were with me. An old lady was lying on the couch, and I could see she was sick.

I introduced myself, still unsure if I should be there or if they needed my help. I said, "I'm a pastor at a local church. I'm not sure if you need our help, but we can pray for your healing. We also have these groceries with us that we are happy to give you."

When I said that, the old woman started crying. She said, "Pastor, I can't believe this, because I prayed to God for two weeks now to somehow help me with groceries. I'm stuck lying on this couch because I'm sick, and there is no way for me to go to the store to buy food. I knew that the days were coming when I would have nothing in my fridge or my pantry to cook for myself and this child."

I was just a random person she had never seen before, but she knew God was using me and my team to answer her prayers for groceries. That was phenomenal for me. I was inspired and reminded that God is a good Father. Sometimes I hear people say, "You don't know my situation. I'm not sure that God or anyone can help me." This sick woman's testimony proves that it doesn't matter what your situation is or what you're going through. God knows exactly where you are, He knows exactly how to help you, and He will do so if you ask Him. He has promised in His Word, "I will not leave you. I will not forsake you. I love you." You are His creation, and He wants to help you.

Sometimes we think God is delayed, but He is never late. Like in the story of this lady, God answered her prayers right on time. She prayed for two weeks, but we came to her house just when she needed help the most. It really encouraged me to see how God answered that woman's prayers and took care of her.

Another story about the personal impact of our ministry comes from a family from Broska village. Let me give you some background. Izmail is currently host to more than 50,000 internally displaced people, and not all of them can live in the city. Lodging is expensive and rental places are hard to find because there are so many people coming here. As a result, people are moving to suburban villages around my city. Broska is one of those villages.

There was a Sunday service when I announced that we were going to have a summer camp on our church property for youth. I told the congregation, "For those of you who are guests here in our city [we don't call them refugees; we call them guests] we don't want to charge you. We know what you are going through. We want to bless you. You can sign your kids up for free."

A lady I already knew came to me after the service. I knew she was staying at a village outside of the city. She said, "Pastor, I would love for my kids to be a part of your summer camp. They would be really happy to go. We are staying in the village of Broska, but I can't afford a round-trip bus ticket for all five of my kids for the five days of your camp. I know you have a church van, and if you are able to drive my children to your summer camp, that would be such a great blessing. They would be so happy. That's the only chance for them to be a part of this camp."

I thought to myself, *That means that another volunteer or I will have to get to their village every day to pick them up and drive them to church. Then in five hours, after the camp is over, we'll have to drive them back to the village, and then drive ourselves all the way back to the church. We are already stretched in so many directions. We don't really have time to do that.*

I was ready to say, "It's not going to work this time. Let's try the next time." When I was about to say this, the Lord spoke to me again, and He said, "Alex, in this case, they have to be part of this."

That was a burden on me, but I responded, *Okay, God, we're busy, but if You really mean that, we will do it.* I told the woman we would ferry her children to and from summer camp.

I drove them personally for the first three days. On the first day, as I was driving them back to the village, I started talking with the 15-year-old elder daughter. We talked about many different things. Then I asked her, "Can you remind me where you are from originally?"

She pronounced the name of the city, and I said, "I don't know where that is. Is that Donetsk or is that Luhansk area? Can you specify?"

When I said that, she started crying. I thought maybe talking about her city had brought up bad memories. Maybe her city had been turned to ashes, and that made her cry, or maybe thinking about her city reminded her about everything her family had lost. I tried to calm her by saying, "I'm sorry. It's okay. Don't cry. It's all right now."

But she said, "Pastor, you don't understand. I can't lie to you any longer."

I was confused: "What do you mean?"

She cried and said, "I feel that I have to tell you the truth. My family is not from the east. We are not internally displaced refugees. In fact, we have lived our whole lives in this village you are driving us back and forth from."

I was less upset than curious as to what was going on. We had been supplying their family for months. They had come to our church claiming they were internally displaced and required help. "So," I said, "can you share with me the rest of the story? Why did you tell this to us? What happened?"

She said that when the war hit the country, many businesses were shut down. Both of her parents lost their jobs. They ended up struggling to feed their five children. Recently, they heard that a church in the city—our church—was giving out supplies, food, and medication to the internally displaced. They thought this was their chance to survive. They told us they were internally displaced, coming from a destroyed city.

The girl said, "You've been taking care of us all this time. You have provided for us, and now we've become a part of your summer camp. I heard what the teachers at Sunday School taught us. I learned about the Ten Commandments and about God. I heard about Jesus and His love. I'm not sure what's going on, but I feel that I can't lie to you any longer. I feel that I want to tell you the truth."

Go Back

When she said this to me, I realized why God wanted me to drive these kids, why He said they had to be a part of the summer camp. I was reminded that our ministry is not only about providing meals, food, and supplies. I knew this before, but this was a good reminder for me, that first of all, our ministry is about reaching the soul. It's about the transformation of people's minds and hearts and drawing them closer to Jesus. I'm positive that the girl was hesitating because she was worried that if she told the truth, we would stop supplying food for her family. But because of what she had learned in church, she preferred to tell the truth and accept the consequences rather than continue to lie. She decided to walk the path of righteousness.

That was such a powerful story for me. While I was rejoicing about this girl's willingness to tell the truth, at the same time I felt so bad knowing that I was living in a country during the days when sometimes people had a hard time just getting food for their children. Why did the girl's parents have to do all these things just to feed their children? I think this testimony encapsulates the situation in our country, for those people on the outside who think it's not that bad.

CHAPTER 9

REFLECTIONS

ON THE WAR

The history of Russia and Ukraine is a long and contentious one. My wife and I are still learning our history because some of what we were told was state-controlled. Some people say that Ukraine is the brother of Russia. If that's true, then we're the youngest brother that Russia has never treated well.

As the rationale for starting the war, Vladimir Putin often says that he invaded to protect Russian-speaking people in Ukraine. He has been quoted several times saying Russian-speaking people are being oppressed, persecuted, and mistreated here. That is simply not true. I have the confidence to say that because I am a Russian-speaking Ukrainian. I'm originally from the very south of the Odessa region, which is predominantly Russian-speaking. Since the war started, I know many people are trying to switch to speaking Ukrainian, but that's another subject.

I have spoken Russian all my life. I have traveled all around Ukraine—north to south, west to east—for the ministry and with my family on vacation. I've been all over Ukraine, and everywhere I went, I spoke Russian. I have never felt any oppression or mistreatment because of my language. As a matter of fact, I spent New Year's in 2022 celebrating with my friend in Lviv. Lviv is famous all around the country as a very Ukrainian city. People mainly speak Ukrainian there. They're very patriotic. I've heard a lot of talk that there are many people in patriotic cities like Lviv who don't like Russian-speaking people, and that you can get in trouble if you speak Russian there.

I experimented with that preconception when I visited Lviv. I can speak Ukrainian, but I spoke only Russian while I was there. I was surprised that I never encountered any oppression, even in Lviv; people were kind and friendly. As long as you are a good and normal person, it's fine. Nobody will mistreat you. Nobody will do anything wrong to you because of the language you speak.

It's ironic that the people who have suffered most in this war are the Russian-speaking people Putin claims he wants to protect. The Russians are fighting in the eastern area of Ukraine and destroying the cities there. That part of Ukraine is a predominantly Russian-speaking area, and those people are really suffering because of Putin's bombs and missiles and because of how the Russian soldiers treat civilians there. The reality is that rather than liberating Russian-speaking people, Putin is causing them more harm and suffering.

I want to be clear that I have no hatred for the Russian people. I don't know what they hope to accomplish through all the violence and destruction, but I don't hate them. Back when I started at a Bible college in Pershotravensk, near Dnipro in the east of Ukraine—an area which is almost totally Russian-speaking—we had around 350 students. I would estimate that around 60% of them were from Russia. I related freely with them and still have friendly relations with some of them.

In my experience, the Ukrainian people were never against Russia. The only thing we wanted was to be a sovereign, independent country, able to build our economy and free to have a relationship with the West—the United States and Europe. Unfortunately, propaganda on Russian media made them think that Ukrainians were Nazis, that we didn't like them, and that we wanted to join the European Union and subscribe to a U.S. agenda to destroy Russia.

Sadly (and I hope that I am wrong), I think this war will go long term, especially if our army does not get the weapons that our president and our minister of defense are appealing to other governments to provide. I believe that because I don't think anything will change Putin's course of action. I think he's a mentally ill person who has an agenda to reconquer Ukraine and reincorporate all the countries from the former Soviet Union back into Russia. I don't believe he appreciates or values the lives of his people or his soldiers. He has an idea, and he's ready to lose everything trying to achieve it. I think the only way for this war to stop is for Ukraine to get its victory.

In addition to that, I personally don't believe that it is a war only between Ukraine and Russia. It is a war of Russia against humanity, against the entire world, and against Christianity. That's what I believe as a Christian. Some people mistakenly think that if Ukraine would just surrender, then there would be no more victims of the war and Putin would stop. I doubt that. He has an imperialistic mindset and an agenda to conquer other nations. If he could overcome Ukraine, or if Ukraine surrenders, that would make him bolder and stronger. That would make him feel like he was invincible and could do whatever he wanted, including recapturing Poland and the Baltic states of Latvia, Lithuania, and Estonia. That's what he wants, and that's what is talked about on their state-controlled media. The propaganda narrative they push on their people is that Ukraine and these other countries are enemies of Russia, so they must be conquered.

That's why I say that this is Putin's war against the whole world. He simply started with Ukraine, and these days, Ukraine stands as a living shield between civilizations. Ukraine stands between democracy and the dictatorship of a godless nation. That's why it's very important for other countries to support and help Ukraine defeat Russia.

You may ask why I claim this is a Russian war against Christianity. This is because in the conquered areas in my country, pastors of Protestant churches are being killed. The Russians are taking church buildings and turning them into storage facilities. They're persecuting Protestant ministers and pastors because they think that if we are not of the Russian Orthodox faith, then we are connected with the U.S.—and they consider the U.S. an enemy. That's why I think it is fair to say this is a war against civilization, democracy, and Christianity, and why the results have an impact far beyond the borders of Ukraine.

As I was writing this book, Russia targeted

their missiles at a huge market, something like a large Home Depot in Ukraine. They launched missiles there during the daytime when people were shopping, and there were at least 23 deaths and 50 people who were badly injured. My sister, who was in Ukraine with her husband, went to Odessa to visit their friends one day. She sent me videos of how drones and missiles attacked Odessa during the night. They couldn't sleep. They prayed because they saw our antimissile defense system shooting down those drones. These are only two examples of the destruction, violence, and fear the war has unleashed on our country.

Some people mistakenly think that the war is no longer as bad as it was in March or April of 2022. Some may think hostilities have almost come to an end, but that's not true. Russia is still attacking Ukraine with missiles, bombs, drones, and soldiers every day, and every day people suffer and die. But I wanted to share the stories in this book with you because it encourages me to recount God's gracious protection through His miraculous intervention. He's proving to be a good Father who is taking care of His children even while a war is raging in our country. He really cares; He really helps. And now I ask that you also care and help us in our time of need.

HOW YOU CAN HELP

I wrote this book because I wanted people to read these stories and be inspired. You may be thinking, *How can a war so devastating and unjust prove the goodness of God?* That is a good question, and one that has been debated for many centuries: how can a good God permit evil to exist? As a pastor, I have been able to witness firsthand the fallen nature of people. Sin has affected every area of our existence, including how nations relate to each other. Very often, the strife caused by sin has resulted in hatred, wars, and bloodshed. God does not endorse any of that but directs His people, who have come to a saving knowledge of Jesus Christ, to overcome the evil by doing good. Romans 12:21 says, "Do not be overcome by evil, but overcome evil with good" (NIV).

Jesus came proclaiming the kingdom of God, and stated at His trial, where He Himself was unjustly treated by the Roman officials, that His kingdom was not of this world. At the same time, He said He wanted His followers to be *in* the world but not *of* it. We are therefore working to establish His kingdom now, just as He taught us to pray: "Your kingdom come, your will be done, on earth as it is in heaven" (Matthew 6:9, NIV).

God wants His people to represent Him in the midst of injustice by showing mercy, kindness, and forgiveness because "The Lord is not slow in keeping his promise, as some understand slowness. Instead, he is patient with you, not wanting anyone to perish, but everyone to come to repentance" (2 Peter 3:9, NIV). Some people are not ready to come to the truth until they have their fill of lies. Some are not ready to turn to God until they have seen what it's like without Him. This war has created a lot of suffering, and some may blame God. Others realize that this is people's doing, and they turn to God for answers.

It was the power of obedience and prayer that has made, and will continue to make, a difference in people's lives. We have seen firsthand how important prayer is. For us, it's been more important than money. Through the power of prayer, our church and our ministry have been protected, and we have been able to adapt to changing needs. I attribute everything our ministry has accomplished to the power of obedience and the power of prayer. All the stories I have shared with you have shown that God is gracious and willing to help in our time of need.

If your heart has been stirred for the people of Ukraine, there are many ways to help. There are people and organizations who are collecting furniture and other things and sending containers to Ukraine. You can donate supplies, give money, or pray. It doesn't have to be a contribution to my ministry specifically.

Go Back

I regularly meet people who are working in different cities and villages. Every time I meet them, all I can do is thank them from the bottom of my heart. It doesn't matter where people are helping in Ukraine because the need is everywhere. I'm really grateful to each missionary, missions organization, and church that is taking trips to Ukraine, no matter to what location. I'm also grateful for all the relief and missions work because it all really helps the people here.

If you feel led to support our church's ministry of preaching the gospel to and providing for the internally displaced people of Ukraine, we would be very grateful. Our Cash App and Zelle information is listed at the end of this section. I can transfer the funds from those platforms to our bank account, and then I can cash it in Ukraine and use the money to buy food and supplies for the ministry.

If you have connections with politicians from your state, please urge them and anyone you know to support the Ukrainian cause. I believe every voice is valuable, and everyone can make a difference. Please speak about Ukraine and make it known to your officials that you will appreciate their support of Ukraine. In these days, we need all the friends we can find. Most importantly, please keep us in your prayers.

AUTHOR'S CONTACT INFORMATION

Cash App: $Alexilash

Zelle: alexilash@gmail.com

YouTube: Pastor Alexander Ilash, @wlwchurch

Facebook: https://www.facebook.com/alexilash.jr

All proceeds from the sale of this book go toward
helping the people of Ukraine.

Made in United States
North Haven, CT
07 November 2024